HORSEPOWER

The Wonder of Draft Horses

by Cris Peterson

Photographs by Alvis Upitis

BOYDS MILLS PRESS

ACKNOWLEDGMENTS
There are many breeds of draft horses, three of which are featured in this book:
Percherons, Belgians, and Clydesdales.
Thanks to the Dennis Oehrlein and Don Parker families who shared their
Percherons, the Bruce Coen family who shared their Belgians,
and to the David Stalheim family who shared their Clydesdales.
Thanks also to Bob and Helen Blomberg, on whose farm the draft horse field day
was held and to Allen Erickson for his interest and support.

AUTHOR'S NOTE
"Horsepower" is a measurement of machine power first introduced to help people
understand the amount of work done by new industrial machines.
One horsepower is the amount of force required to pull a weight of
150 pounds out of a hole 220 feet deep in one minute.

Text copyright © 1997 by Cris Peterson
Photographs copyright © 1997 by Alvis Upitis

Published by Caroline House
Boyds Mills Press, Inc.
A Highlights Company
815 Church Street
Honesdale, PA 18431
Printed in China

Publisher Cataloging-in-Publication Data
Peterson, Cris.
Horsepower : the wonder of draft horses / by Cris Peterson ;
photographs by Alvis Upitis.—1st ed.
[32]p. : col. ill. ; cm.
Summary : Draft horses, such as Clydesdales, Percherons, and Belgians, are described in words
and pictures and shown to be powerful co-workers on farms, past and present.
ISBN 1-56397-626-9   Hardcover
ISBN 1-56397-943-8   Paperback
1. Horses—Juvenile literature. 2. Draft horses—Juvenile literature. [1. Horses 2. Draft horses.]
I. Upitis, Alvis, ill. II. Title
636.1'5—dc20   1997   AC   CIP
Library of Congress Catalog Card Number 96-84679

First edition, 1997
First Boyds Mills Press paperback edition, 2001
Book designed by Amy Drinker, Aster Designs
The text of this book is set in 15-point New Century Schoolbook.

10 9 8 7 6 5 4 3 2   Hardcover
10 9 8 7 6 5 4 3 2 1   Paperback

For my parents, Carmen and Bill Hoeppner.
— C.P.

*For my dad, who showed me the value of work,
and shares the joy of photography.*
— A.U.

Keane and MacKenzie own a most remarkable horse named Kate. Her huge black hooves are the size of dinner plates. She is as tall as a basketball player and weighs as much as a class-room of first-graders. Kate is a Percheron draft horse.

One hundred years ago, draft horses like Kate clip-clopped on every city street and country road in America. Before there were cars or trucks, horses pulled carriages full of people and wagons full of milk. Before there were tractors or combines, horses pulled plows through spring sod and corn pickers through fall fields. Some twenty-seven million draft horses were America's main source of power.

Kate is much bigger than a ranch horse or a racehorse.
She is descended from the giant war horses used by
soldiers in times of castles, kings, and knights in armor.
Her broad chest and strong legs allow her to pull
tremendous loads. When you stand near a horse like
Kate, you can sense her intelligence and feel her gentle-
ness and power.

Instead of a saddle, Kate wears a harness when she works. A carefully fitted collar of leather and wood rests on her shoulders. A pair of shiny metal hames nestle into grooves on the collar. Leather straps called traces are attached to the hames at one end and to whatever Kate is pulling at the other. More lines and leather straps fit together, allowing Keane and MacKenzie to control Kate.

$\mathbf{P}$eople who love working with draft horses have kept these amazing animals from disappearing. Some farmers still plow fields with horses. Matched teams with fancy harnesses trundle down city streets during parades. And in some regions of the country, Amish farmers still use horses like Kate for all their field work.

Draft horse enthusiasts often attend special field days. Owners demonstrate how well their teams work together and share information and stories about their horses. Keane and MacKenzie and some of their friends recently attended such a field day.

Don's team of Percherons wears bright red harness pads for the field day. The team pulls a mechanical corn picker and later demonstrates plowing. Don remembers when his father used horses on the family farm fifty years ago. Now each spring Don prepares his Percherons

for field work. It takes about thirty minutes to harness and hitch a team of four.

On a breezy morning, Don's team joins two smaller teams for a day of plowing. In the teams of three, the horses work side by side. In Don's team of four, the lead horses—Bill and Bob—are older and more experienced. They need to be half a step faster than the wheel horses behind them so all the traces remain taut.

When Don's team turns at the end of the field, it's a sight to see. In a great lumbering, jangling dance, the lead horses sidestep in careful time with their teammates, throwing up clods of soil behind them. The ground shakes as the wheel horses prance in place, slowly turning themselves around. Every half hour or so, the team rests at the end of the field.

Bruce and his family raise Belgian draft horses on their farm. At the field day, he hitches twelve horses behind a four-bottom plow. A dozen Belgians working together create an impressive, powerful team.

Nearly all of Bruce's horses have been bred from one special mare named Bonnie. Although Bonnie has been blind over half her life, she is Bruce's lead mare. With one ear turned to listen, she follows each command: "Come around, Bonnie...*hup, hup...hup* now, Bonnie...*whoa*."

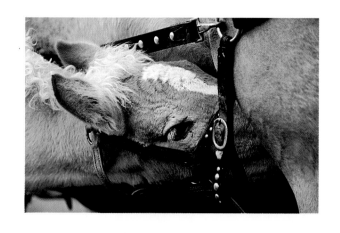

In the spring and early summer, Bruce's mares give birth to tawny, curly-haired foals. Major was born a month ago. He has learned to lead and be tied up, but his favorite activity is taking a snack from his mother. Already he is over four feet tall at the shoulders and can look his young visitor in the eye.

David and his family raise Clydesdale draft horses. The distinctive feathering on the horses' long legs makes them very showy. At the field day, David's horses pull wagonloads of corn and demonstrate plowing.

David shows his Clydesdales at regional and national conferences. It takes a year of work on the farm before the drafters are ready for showing. All winter long, Warrior, Patrick, and several other horses go through "basic training" on a daily schedule. They learn to stand at attention, heads high and hooves together. They will compete in halter and hitch competitions, where they are judged on appearance and on how well they work together as a team.

A month before a show, shoes are put on the horses' hooves to keep them smooth and trimmed. Fifteen year-old Andrew, who has worked with his dad's Clydesdales nearly all his life, now has the job of shoeing the show horses. His horse patiently stands on three legs while Andrew nails on a shoe. Then they head down the driveway for a trial run to check that the shoes fit properly.

For hundreds of years
draft horses like Kate,
Bonnie, and Warrior
pulled sleighs and wagons, plows and pickers as they
helped build our country and produce our food. Today
it's hard to imagine a time when "horsepower" meant
horses working.

But there are still some farms where you can hear the jingling of harnesses and the soft nicker of draft horses working in partnership with their owners.